LONG, LONG, LONG AGO

by Gerry Bailey

illustrated by
Steve Boulter and Jan Smith

Reading Adviser:
Susan Kesselring, M.A., Literacy Educator
Rosemount-Apple Valley-Eagan
(Minnesota) School District

PICTURE WINDOW BOOKS
www.picturewindowbooks.com

First American edition published in 2005 by
Picture Window Books
5115 Excelsior Boulevard
Suite 232
Minneapolis, MN 55416
877-845-8392
www.picturewindowbooks.com

Publisher: Felicia Law

Design director: Tracy Carrington

Project manager: Karen Foster

Author: Gerry Bailey

Editors: Rosalind Beckman, Christianne Jones,
and Jackie Wolfe

Designed by: Jacqueline Palmer; assisted by Fanny
Level, Will Webster, and Tracy Davies

Cartoon illustrations: Steve Boulter (Advocate)
and Andrew Keylock (Specs Art Agency)

Make-and-do: Jan Smith

Model-maker: Tim Draper
further models: Robert Harvey, Abby Dean

Photo studio: Steve Lumb

Photo research: Diana Morris

Scanning: Acumen Colour

Proof-reading: Victoria Grimsell

Digital workflow: Edward MacDermott

Library of Congress Cataloging-in-Publication Data
Bailey, Gerry.
Long, long ago / written by Gerry Bailey ;
illustrated by Steve Boulter and Jan Smith.
p. cm. — (Crafty inventions)
Includes bibliographical references (p.   ).
ISBN 1-4048-1043-9 (hardcover : alk. paper)
1. Technology—Juvenile literature. 2. Inventions—
Juvenile literature. I. Boulter, Steve, ill. II. Smith,
Jan, ill. III. Keylock, Andrew, ill. IV. Title. V. Series.

T48.B144 2004
600—dc22   2004024440

Photo Credits

H. & J. Blackwell/Trip: 17t. Steve Brock/Eye
Ubiquitous: 30b.; James Davis Travel
Photography: 29t.; J. Ellard/Trip: 38b.; P. M.
Field/Eye Ubiquitous: 9t.; W. Jacobs/Trip: 26b.;
Darren Maybury/Eye Ubiquitous: 33t.; John
Miles/Eye Ubqiuitous: 37t.; Brian
Mitchell/Photofusion: 14t.; Gianni Dagli
Orti/Corbis: 42b.; Chris Parker/Hutchison
Picture Library: 21t.; Topham Picturepoint: 22b.;
Picturesque/Trip: 10b.; Roger Ressmeyer/Corbis:
13t.; H. Rogers/Trip: 5t. Paul Seheult/Eye
Ubqiuitous: 34b.; Dr Nigel Smith/Hutchison: 25t.
G Stokoe/Trip: 18b.; Trip: 41t. Graham
Wheatley/Eye Ubiquitous: 6b.

Crafty Inventions

LONG, LONG, AGO

Table of Contents

What Can I Use to Hunt the Lion?

Belo the hunter is hungry. He needs to go out hunting, except there is nothing around to hunt. Everything has been chased away by a lion. Belo has to do something about the lion, but how can he hunt and kill such a dangerous beast?

Belo looks at his hunting equipment—a few stones and a small stick he throws at animals. He is used to driving some animals over cliffs as well. But there are no animals to chase.

The lion is a dangerous beast. How can Belo get close enough to throw a rock at it? And he dare not miss. Perhaps he could sharpen his stick. But then he'd have to get even closer.

I'm so hungry. How can I catch some food without the lion catching me?

WHAT CAN HE DO?

- Dress up and paint his face, then try to frighten the lion away. But lions aren't afraid of much.

- Dig a pit and lure the lion into it with some bait. But he has no bait— except himself. That's no good.

- Sharpen his stick and get close enough to throw it. Pretty dangerous. And would the stick be sharp enough, anyway?

- What if he used his flint knife to throw at the lion? That's a good idea because it's sharp. But it won't fly through the air easily.

I'll put the two ideas together to make a throwing blade called a spear. I'll cut a notch at one end of my stick and fit the flint blade into the notch. I'll bind it tightly with grass twine. Now I can hunt the lion from a safe distance.

Later, spearheads like these were made of bronze.

Spearheads

In prehistoric times, people made **spears** and arrowheads from sharpened **flint** stones. The flint head was tied to a long wooden pole, or shaft, with cord. The spear could be thrown a great distance because of its **aerodynamic** shape. Hunters used their spears to hunt wild animals.

These included large cats, wild boar, reindeer, bison, and elk. Spear-throwing became a skill the hunter had to master at a young age. Later, spears were used in battle, for both attack and defense. A soldier holding a spear could keep an enemy at more than an arm's length away.

Aerodynamics

Aerodynamics is the study of the forces that act on an object as it moves through the air. It is important to designers and engineers working on moving things such as airplanes, rockets, and cars.

When an object moves through air, the air rubs against it. This rubbing, called **friction**, slows the object down. Scientists and engineers try to overcome friction by designing objects that rub as little as possible on the air. An object that reduces friction in this way is called aerodynamic.

An airplane is very aerodynamic. Its sharp, pointed nose allows it to cut through the atmosphere easily. The nose of the plane pushes the air aside so friction is reduced. The smooth metal surface of the plane makes sure that friction is reduced even more.

RACING CARS

The first racing cars were not very aerodynamic. They were too bulky at the front. Today's racing cars use aerodynamics to create smooth shapes that cut through the air. To achieve the best shape possible, racing cars are sent to special wind tunnels for testing.

Inventor's words

aerodynamic
flint
friction
spear
wind tunnel

This airplane has an aerodynamic shape. The front is wedge-shaped to reduce friction. The sides are smooth, which also reduces friction.

Make your own aerodynamic spears

You will need
- paper • scissors
- glue
- paint

1 Cut a thin strip of paper about 1.6 inches (4 cm) wide.

2 Take a piece of paper about 8 inches (20 cm) by 4 inches (10 cm) and fold it in half to make a square. Glue the thin strip to the inside so the long tail sticks out.

3 Fold the square to make a paper dart (the spearhead), with the thin strip as the spear handle inside. Glue together.

4 Paint and decorate your collection of aerodynamic spears and darts.

5 You can experiment with different shapes of darts and different lengths of tails to find out which designs fly best. Try adding a paper clip to the nose to balance the flight.

How Can I Pull a Heavy Sled?

Indo is a hunter. He drags a sled with him on the hunt so he can bring the animals back home. But today is different. He has fallen and injured his leg. It is too dangerous to leave him because there are wild animals around. Lea, his wife, must put Indo on the sled and pull him home instead.

The sled is impossible to push. What can I use to help move my heavy husband?

Lea tries to push the sled. But with Indo on top, it's too heavy and won't budge.

WHAT CAN SHE DO?

- Tell Indo to hop home as fast as he can and hope the wild animals are slower and better fed than he is.

- How about raiding a beehive for the honey, then spreading a slippery path and sliding Indo home? But she'd be stung!

- Roll the sled home over some logs. She'd need quite a few, but rolling sounds good.

- What if she used some short pieces of log instead of large, heavy ones, to move the sled along?

8

I'll chop narrow circles from the logs, because circles will roll along the ground. If I attach them under the sled, one at each corner, they'll move both the sled and the load. Then I'll fix the circles so they can spin around easily on a short pole.

A Chinese horsecart with solid wheels is still used in some parts of China.

Early wheels

A **wheel** is a round **disc**. It spins, or rotates, around a pole called an **axle**, which is attached through the center point of the disc. The idea of the wheel probably developed from the use of rolling logs to carry loads. As the load moved forward, the back log would be rushed to the front. Progress was very slow. When disc-shaped wheels were attached to a platform under the load, a huge leap forward in the history of transportation was made. These wheels were heavy, but they cut down even more on **friction**. This made pulling a load much easier for humans and beasts.

Friction

It is hard work dragging a heavy object such as a sled. The sled rubs against the rough surface of the ground underneath. This rubbing is caused by a force called friction. Friction is produced when two objects touch or rub against each other.

Friction is a force that tries to slow moving things down. It also tries to stop still things from starting to move in the first place. Any object that is moving or beginning to move will feel friction. But there is less friction between smooth surfaces than between rough surfaces. Skates, for example, glide easily over smooth ice, while the textured tread on tires grips rough roads.

A dogsled can carry a heavy load because the runners glide over smooth snow, which reduces the friction.

RUBBING TOGETHER

When two surfaces are pressed together, some of the atoms in each surface mix together, or "weld." When we try to move the two surfaces against each other, we have to break those "welds." The force that tries to stop us from doing this is called friction.

Inventor's words

atom
axle
disc
friction
wheel

Make a model cart

You will need

- a small box or food tub about 6 inches (15 cm) x 2.8 inches (7 cm)
- two small round foil baking tins
- sticky tape
- two pins or thumbtacks
- two small pieces of cork or foam packaging
- a small stick or wooden skewer
- string or twine
- paint and paintbrush

1 Cut the box down to make a shallow container, and decorate it with paint.

2 Make the wheels by flattening the baking tins and sticking tape on one side to reinforce the center. Alternatively, you could cut out wheels from a piece of cardboard.

3 Pin the wheels to the cart with the pins or thumbtacks on the outside and the cork on the inside.

4 Push a length of skewer into the base of the box and secure with tape. Tie a shorter stick on to make a crossbar.

5 You can add a piece of cardboard to make a floor inside. Load your wagon with straw or raffia.

How can I Lift the Huge Stones?

The ancient priest Corpulent is puzzled. He and his men have dragged huge stones called megaliths over many miles. Now they are lodged upright in the ground. But the men don't know how to finish the monument. They cannot raise the huge stones that go on top.

Corpulent wants to build a monument that's bigger and better than any seen before. He will lay stones called lintels on top of the megaliths.

But the stones are huge and incredibly heavy. No one has the muscle to perform this mammoth task.

How can I raise the heavy lintels and place them securely across the top of the megaliths?

WHAT CAN HE DO?

- Make wooden blocks and paint them to look like rock and hope the high priest won't notice.

- What if he hauled the lintels into place using ropes? Pulling with ropes might work if his men can take the strain.

- He could use as many men as possible to make a human slope or ramp. Good idea, but what about his men? They'd be crushed!

- Slide the lintels up a wooden ramp? Hmm! But it might work if the ramp is strong enough.

I'm sure the ramp will work, but it'll have to be strong, so I'm going to build one made of tightly packed earth. Then I can pull the lintels up the earth ramp and slide them into place on top of the standing stones.

Scientists believe that earth ramps were used in the building of Stonehenge in Britain more than 3,500 years ago.

Earth ramp

An earth **ramp** is a solid, sloping surface made of earth, or rocks and earth tightly packed together. Since it is solid and therefore very sturdy, it can support very heavy weights. Earth ramps were used to help build many ancient buildings and **monuments**.

The ancient Egyptians built earth ramps to raise the huge blocks of stone that formed the pyramids. Early engineers used smaller earth ramps to haul **lintel** stones and ease them into place across two standing **megaliths**.

Ramps

A ramp is a sloping surface linking two places that are at different levels. A ramp is also known as an inclined plane.

Imagine a heavy barrel that needs to be lifted up to a high rack. You might be able lift the barrel straight up if you were very strong. But this would be hard work. Your muscle power would have to match the barrel's weight, or **load**.

Instead, you could roll the barrel up a ramp. Using a ramp is easier because the weight of thc force needed is much less than the load. The barrel may need to be pushed a longer distance, but because the load is lighter, pushing it a bit further is well worth it.

SKATEBOARD

Skateboarders sometimes use a ramp to give them more speed. The ramp works to reduce the upward force of the ground beneath. This allows gravity to pull skateboarders down along the ramp. The steeper the ramp, the faster they are pulled down.

Inventor's words

gravity
inclined plane
lintel • load
megalith
monument
ramp

A ramp helps a wheelchair user to reach the same level as a person using steps.

Make a working force-measurer

You will need
- board about 20-28 in (50-70 cm) long
- pencil • ruler
- drinking straw
- rubber band
- thin skewer or straightened wire coat hanger
- toothpick • pin
- small toy truck, filled with sand or gravel
- string

1 Mark a scale on the board using a pencil and ruler.

2 Cut a length of drinking straw about 1.2 inches (3 cm) long. Push the rubber band through it, using the skewer or wire hanger.

3 Make a pinhole through the straw, then push the toothpick through so it holds one end of the rubber band. Attach the other end of the rubber band to the board with the pin or thumbtack.

4 Attach a string loop to the front of the truck, then hook this on to the toothpick.

WHAT HAPPENS?

As you raise the board and make the ramp steeper, you can measure the force that the truck puts on the rubber band. If you hold the board upright, the truck pulls the rubber band right down. As you lower the board to make a ramp, it gradually pulls the truck up more easily as the ramp becomes less steep.

How Can I Plant My Seeds?

Farmer Ham has a big field to plant and a lot of seeds to sow. But the ground in the field is hard, and the seeds just lie on the surface when he throws them down. He needs to get the seeds into the rich soil if they are to grow well.

First, Ham uses a pointed stick to make holes in the ground into which he can drop the seeds. But it takes far too long and is tiring. The field is just too big.

Then Ham tries to stamp the seeds into the ground. But the earth is too hard and the seeds split or roll away. Some are stolen by the crows that watch and wait for easy pickings.

How can I plant my seeds deep enough to get the better of those pesky crows?

WHAT CAN HE DO?

- Ask the crows to help him. They can use their beaks to peck holes in the ground. But they'd probably eat most of the seed while they were at it!

- Scratching furrows with his fingers might work. The rows would be nice and straight, but not very deep. His fingers would ache.

- What if he used a flat stick to scrape out a furrow in the ground? But sticks would soon become blunt or snap against the hard earth.

- An axe might be better. The furrows would be deeper, which is good, but it would be back-breaking work!

I've got a brilliant idea! I'll tie a large cutting blade behind my ox and use it to carve out a deep, straight furrow. I'll make sure that the ditch is the same depth all along its length. Then, as I walk behind the ox, I'll scatter seeds into the furrows.

A plow pulled by a water buffalo cuts into a watery paddy in China. Plows such as these are still used in parts of China.

The first plow

A **plow** is a machine that prepares land ready for seeds to be sown. It has a handle for steering and a **blade** that acts as a **wedge**. The blade digs into the soil, loosening it and turning it over. Modern plows often have many rows of steel blades and are usually pulled by large tractors.

The first plows were probably used in China and parts of the Middle East. They were pulled by oxen and cut grooves called **furrows** into the soil. Similar horse-drawn plows are still used today. The farmer guides the plow with a handle to make sure that the furrows are straight.

The wedge

A wedge is a simple machine. It is used to push and spread things apart.

The blade of an **axe** is a type of wedge. When the cutting edge is driven into a log, the powerful movement creates a strong force that splits open the wood. The downward effort of the hand is changed into a sideways splitting effort that cuts the log.

SCISSOR BLADES

Most of the machines we use are made up of combinations of simple devices. An everyday example is the scissors. Each blade of the scissors is a wedge. But the two blades, or wedges, are joined to make another device—a lever—which gives the scissors an even stronger cutting action.

Any sharp object is a type of wedge—knives, arrows, or needles are all wedges. The sharp **bow** of a ship acts as a wedge when it moves through the water. The pointed end of a rocket cuts through the air as it powers through the atmosphere.

A Vietnamese woman chopping wood.

Inventor's words

axe • blade • bow
furrow • lever
plow • wedge

Make a traditional plow

You will need

- marker • scissors
- acrylic paint
- empty square-shaped plastic container, like a milk or household cleaner bottle
- strong glue to stick plastic
- forked twig (like the one in the picture), and some small straight twigs
- different kinds of string, or thin strips of leather or plastic

1 Draw the shape of the plow blade with a marker around the corner of the plastic container

2 Cut out carefully with scissors. Then do exactly the same on the other side of the container. Now glue the two blades together.

3 Tie the plow blade to the twig so that the pointed curve will dig into the soil. Wind the string around and around to make it secure.

4 Make the plow handle by tying a short twig across the end of the plow. Tie another twig at the other end. Attach string or pieces of leather for the ropes to pull the plow.

5 Paint the blade of the plow with acrylic paint.

How Can I Get Water to My Crops?

The Nile River runs through a hot, dry country called Egypt. Each year, the waters of the Nile rise up over its banks to flood the dry land on either side. The water helps the crops grow. But this year the Nile is very low. The water cannot reach the crops.

The waters of the Nile are not rising as usual this year. The soil in Farmer Gamel's field is dry and dusty.

The ditches that carry water through the fields are almost dry. The farmer's crops need water or they will soon wither and die.

How can I get the water up the steep bank to my plants before they die?

Farmer Gamel is worried. The bank is too steep to haul up water.

WHAT CAN HE DO?

- Wait for it to rain. Hmm!

- Slide down the bank and fill his cupped hands with water. Then climb back up to the dry plants. Exhausting!

- Tie a bucket to some rope, lower it into the water, and pull it up full. A bucket's a good idea ...

- Train an elephant to suck up water in its trunk, swing around, and spray the crops. Yes, swinging could work ...

- Tie a bucket to a plank. Dip the plank into the water and then bring it back up.

I know, I'll use a bucket and the swing idea to make a water dipper. I'll make a big lever with a bucket tied to a rope on one end and a weight on the other. I'll call my gadget a shadoof.

The shadoof is still used in parts of Africa and India.

The shadoof

A **shadoof** is a water-raising device first used by the early Egyptians over 2000 years ago. It consists of a bucket-like container made from animal skins or clay that is tied to one end of a **lever**.

The other end of the lever is weighted with heavy stones. The container is dipped into the water. When full, it is lifted up and poured into ditches that carry water to **irrigate** the fields.

Levers

The lever is a simple machine that helps us do many different kinds of work. It is very useful, for example, when we need to lift something that is very heavy.

The most common kind of lever is a straight length of wood, such as a board, that rests or balances on something underneath. The board is called the **arm** and the place where it rests is called the **fulcrum**. Every lever has an arm and a fulcrum.

When you place a **load** on one end of the board, you can lift it more easily by pushing down on the other end. The end of the board, or arm, that you move is called the **force** or **effort** end. This is because you use force or effort to move it. The other end is called the load end because it carries the load that has to be moved.

A seesaw is a type of lever. The fulcrum is the wooden stand in the center. The arm carries the children.

Inventor's words

arm
effort
force • fulcrum
irrigate
lever • load
shadoof

22

Make a working shadoof

You will need

- three sticks about 12 in (30 cm) long
- tray of sand
- one shorter and one longer stick
- toothpick
- plastic cup
- string
- small pebbles

1 Tie the three 12 inch (30 cm) sticks together and stand them in the tray of soil or gravel. Tie a small twig near the top as a rest for the beam.

2 Make the water container by pushing a toothpick through the plastic cup and attaching string loops.

3 Loosely lie the long twig on to the beam-rest. Tie the cup to one end.

4 Tie a couple of pebbles together with string and tie them to the other end of the beam.

You can lower your shadoof over the kitchen sink and use it to raise water.

How Can We Travel on Water?

In prehistoric times, the only way to go from one place to another was to walk or run. This was fine on land. But it was no good if you wanted to cross a river that was fast and deep—especially if you had a heavy load to carry!

Lem and his friends are looking for animals to hunt. Ahead is a deep, wide river. On the far side, a large herd of deer is grazing among the trees. How can the hunters get to the other side?

Even if I get across on a log, how can I bring a deer back?

WHAT CAN THEY DO?

- Brave the strong currents and swim across. But then they need to haul the dead animal back. Not easy!

- What if they each cut down a tree and paddle it across the river? After the hunt, they could tow the dead animal behind them. But the deer might sink.

- How about holding on to each other, and holding on to the logs, and holding on to the deer? How many hands is that?

- They could use ropes of animal skin to tie themselves to the logs, or the deer to the logs—or just the logs to the logs ...

Logs will be useful. We'll cut down some trees and tie the trunks together to make a platform. Then we'll be able to cross the river together, hunt for food, and bring it back on this raft.

A log raft with special fencing is used to carry cattle across a river.

Log raft

The first **rafts** were probably just logs tied together with ropes made of animal skin. Two logs were used as **crossbeams** to **stabilize** the raft at each end. Sometimes, animal skins were **inflated** with air and attached under the raft to make it it more stable.

A stable raft can carry more people or goods. Rafts or flat boats such as these traded along the rivers of the world. In Egypt, long reeds were cut into bundles and fastened together. Later, the reed rafts were shaped and curved. These were the first boats.

Floating

All objects will either float or sink when placed in water. This will depend on both their weight and their size. The combination of the weight and size of an object is called density. Density means how much a certain amount, or volume, of material weighs.

Like all substances, water has density, too. An object that is less dense than the weight of the same amount of water will float. If the object is more dense than the same amount of water, it will sink. A pebble is made up of very dense material that is packed tightly together. Although it is small, it will sink. It weighs far more than the weight of the same, tiny amount of water. It could never float!

A heavy dugout tree trunk will float, even with someone on it, because it is less dense than the water it is floating in.

DISPLACING WATER

A ship floats half in and half out of the water. It is less heavy than the water it has displaced. However, if the ship is loaded with extra goods, it will sink lower and lower. If it becomes heavier than the water it has displaced, the ship will sink.

Inventor's words

crossbeam
density • displace
float • inflate
raft • stabilize
substance
volume

Craft a raft!

You will need

- several sticks or twigs cut to the same length
- string or garden raffia
- scissors
- bowl of water or large shallow dish

1 Line up the sticks so that they form a platform.

2 Use the string to tie the twigs together. The string should go over and under each stick in turn.

3 Now tie together the twigs at the other end in the same way. Take two twigs for the crossbars and trim to size.

4 Attach the crossbars to each end of the platform. Thread the string through the holes between the sticks and secure firmly.

5 Make different items of cargo to carry on the raft.
- A small piece of cloth tied around gravel makes a sack.
- Roll up fabric and tie in a bundle.
- Make a tub full of goods.
- Paint corks to look like barrels. Glue them to stack together.

How Can I Cross the River?

Lamka, the shepherdess, needs to move her flock to a new pasture. But the grassy field lies across a wide, fast-moving stream. Lamka must think up a plan to get to the other side. Would that piece of old wood be of any use?

The piece of wood stretches across the river. The first sheep crosses safely. But the next few sheep to cross make the wood bend in the middle.

How can I make it safe for my sheep to cross the stream to graze?

Lamka decides not to send over any more sheep. She imagines the wood bending so much that it cracks with the weight, carrying her flock into the stream.

WHAT CAN SHE DO?

- She could carry her sheep across one by one.

- What if she used the wood to build a raft to get the sheep across? But they might get seasick!

- How about laying stepping stones across the stream? It would take time to train the sheep to use them. But stones might be useful ...

- She could wade into the stream and support the center of the wood herself, but she'd risk being swept away. Could something else support it?

I'll use the wood to make a bridge and support it by resting it on boulders spaced out across its length. Now it won't bend or break. The boulders will allow the bridge to take the stress of the sheep crossing.

This is a simple bridge, with stone piers for support.

Bridge support

A **bridge** is a **structure** that allows people or vehicles to pass over a river, road, or railway. The very first bridges may have been made from tree trunks. Girder bridges are known to be thousands of years old, and were certainly among the first bridges to have been built.

Most bridges have supports underneath that help to carry the weight of the bridge and whatever moves across it. The supports may be made of wood, stone, or iron. The support, called a **pier**, acts as a **force** against the **stress** on the bridge. Stress can make the bridge bend out of shape or break.

Stress

Stress is a force or pressure. Stress can make an object change its shape. It can squash or compress something, or it can stretch and expand it. When scientists and engineers talk about calculating stress, they are talking about how to measure the pressure being put on something.

If the stress on an object is too great, the object may bend or break. A bench, for example, is usually strong enough to resist the stress of people sitting on it. But if you put a big, heavy elephant on the bench, the stress would be too much. The bench would bend and—more likely—break.

A road bridge under construction. Girders are strong enough to bear the stress caused by the weight of the bridge and the traffic crossing it.

STRESSES AND STRAINS

Stress and strain go together. Strain measures how much the shape of an object changes under stress, or how much it bends. The greater the stress, the greater the strain, and the more an object will bend. Rubber, which bends easily, will show greater strain than a tougher material such as steel.

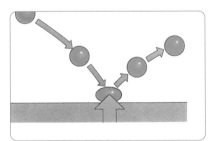

Inventor's words

bridge
compress
expand • force
pier • pressure
strain • stress
structure

Make three different bridges

You will need

- newspaper • glue
- thick cardboard
- paint
- selection of small stones and flat pebbles
- thin cardboard
- wooden toothpicks or skewer sticks
- string • scissors

1 For the landscape, scrunch up the newspaper to make hills and glue to the thick cardboard as shown. Between the hills, paste down newspaper scraps to make a smooth surface for the river. Paint the hills and the river.

GIRDER BRIDGE

To make a beam bridge, fold a narrow strip of thin cardboard lengthways. Cut small rectangles of cardboard and glue to the bridge to make paving slabs. Glue the bridge to the sides of the hill.

SUSPENSION BRIDGE

To make a suspension bridge, cut up or break toothpicks or skewers into 2 in (5 cm) lengths Tie these on to two pieces of string and knot to secure. Tie the ends of the string around large pebbles.

STONE BRIDGE

To make a stone bridge, place small stones on the river for the piers and flat pebbles for the path across.

DID YOU KNOW?

Stone bridges are fine for shallow water.
Suspension bridges need strong anchors at each end.
Girder bridges rest on strong beams.

How Can We Stay Dry and Safe?

Fenel has decided to give up life as a hunter. He's tired of moving around all the time. He wants to settle down and become a farmer. But he will need a place that will protect him and his wife from the rain and cold and from wild animals that prowl around.

In the open there is no protection from hungry lions that creep up on people.

He tries standing branches in front of him, but they just fall down.

How can I shelter and protect myself and my wife from the weather and wild animals?

He must also consider the weather. There are strong winds and rain. Much of the ground will become flooded if the rain continues.

WHAT CAN HE DO?

- Make a pair of stilts and walk around on them. He would be dry and safe from the animals— perhaps ...

- Build a tree house. But his farm animals would have to stay on the ground.

- Make a round fence of wooden stakes and live behind it. He would still get wet and cold, but it might stop the animals from getting in.

- Building an umbrella of leaves over the top of the fence might do it, although the wind would still howl through.

I'll hammer four posts into the ground and make a floor to rest on the posts. Then I'll use four woven fences to make a square building over the raised floor and put a roof of thatched grass on top. Now I have a shelter that will protect us.

Houses built on stilts are found in places where there is danger of flooding.

Safe shelter

The first **buildings** were simple huts in which families, and sometimes their animals, found **shelter**. The frame of the building was made of interwoven branches, animal tusks, or bones. The walls formed a covering for the frame. They were probably first made of skins or grasses.

Later buildings were made of wood. Sometimes larger buildings called **longhouses**, single-roomed buildings longer than they were wide, were made to house whole families. In rainy places, some of these homes were built on **stilts**. Houses like these can still be seen in parts of Asia today.

Buildings

A building is a structure with walls and a roof. The walls of the building support each other. They are strong enough to resist outside forces, such as wind and rain, and to support the roof, which is a heavy load that presses down on the walls.

Modern buildings are made of strong materials that can resist stress from the forces that push against it. These include bricks and mortar—mortar adds great strength to a brick structure. Steel beams, called girders, form a frame around which the walls of the building are fitted. Concrete, a mixture of cement, water and crushed stones, is used to hold the materials together. Piles made of concrete and steel are sunk into holes in the ground to anchor the building.

SWAYING STRUCTURES

Buildings such as skyscrapers have to be strong. But they have to be able to move as well, or they might snap during violent storms. The steel skeleton, or frame, of the building allows it to sway.

Structures such as tall buildings and bridges are constructed with strong materials, including concrete and steel.

Inventor's words

building
concrete
girder
load • longhouse
mortar
shelter • stilts
structure

Make a house on stilts

You will need

- foam packaging, about .4–.8 inches(1–2 cm) thick
- scissors
- thick cardboard from an old carton
- grass, raffia, or dried plant stems
- glue • pins
- four sticks or straight twigs, about pencil thickness
- thin sticks or wooden skewers
- fine string

1 Use scissors to cut the foam into two blocks about 6 x 4 inch (15 x 10 centimeter). These are the base and roof of the hut. Cut pieces of cardboard for the walls and roof of the hut.

2 Decorate the cardboard roof and walls by gluing grass, raffia, or dried stems to cover each piece.

3 Attach the front, back, and sides of the hut with pins pushed into the foam blocks. Glue and pin the roof on top.

4 Push the twigs into the base to make the stilts.

5 Make a ladder with the thin sticks and string.

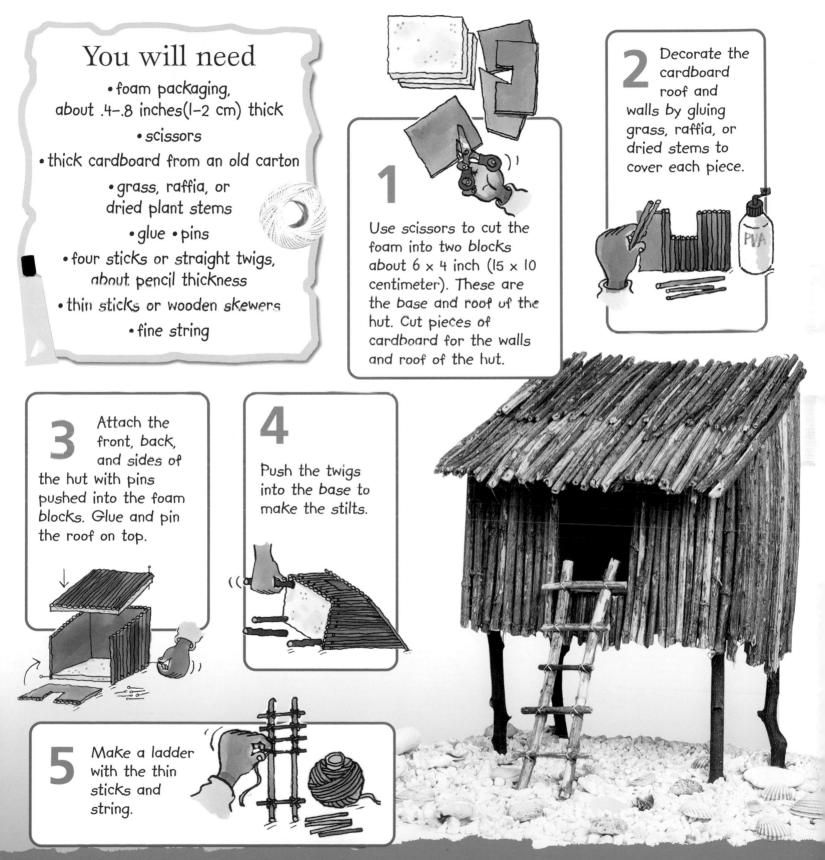

How Can I Paint in Color?

Tribal leader, Awsum, wants a record of his latest victory drawn in color on the cave walls. Yidah, the tribal artist, argues that he always uses charcoal to make his drawings because he has never made a color paint that works. But despite Yidah's protests, the leader insists.

He tries to make colors from crushed rocks, but the powder won't stick to the walls.

He makes other colors from crushed flowers, but they're too pale.

Color would look really good. How can I make color paints that will stick to the wall?

He even tries to paint using the blood of an ox mixed with water, but the blood just dries out and the pictures look cracked and brown.

WHAT CAN HE DO?

- Tell Awsum he is color blind so he can still work with charcoal.

- Create battle pictures with whole flower petals. Colorful but not very heroic. And the flowers will soon rot.

- Make colors from crushed rocks and ram's blood, and hope something sticks. Ugh! The crushed rocks have interesting colors, though.

- He really dislikes using blood. Maybe there's another part of the animal that would work.

I know, what if I mixed crushed rock with animal fat? The two substances will make a greasy paste that'll be easy to use and stick to the wall. When it dries out, it will keep its bright color and thick texture.

A cave painting of a prehistoric fish.

Paste and pigments

Paints are a mixture of dry, colored powder called a **pigment**, and a sticky substance called a **binder**. When the binder dries out, it attaches the pigment to the surface that is being painted. The first pigments, called earth pigments, came from crushed soft rocks or earth that were colored by minerals. **Substances** such as clay and ocher produced reds, yellows, and browns. Charcoal was used to make black. Later, copper oxide was crushed to make green. Mixed together, the pigment and binder produced an oily paint that could be brushed or hand-painted on to a surface.

Affixing paints

Paint is the substance artists use to make a picture. The paint is spread on a surface such as canvas, wood, paper, or stone. Paints are made by mixing dry, powdered colors called pigments with sticky substances called binders. When the sticky binder dries out and hardens, it holds the colored pigment to the surface.

Modern pigments come from earth that has been colored by minerals such as iron, or from materials made in a factory. There are many kinds of binders. Some are vegetable gums such as gum arabic, or vegetable oils such as linseed oil. Egg yolks are also used as a binder. Different binders dry out at different speeds, which affect the shine or texture of a painting. Paint can be made thinner by adding a liquid, such as turpentine.

AIRBRUSH

Some modern painters use a special brush to do their work. In fact, it isn't a brush at all. It's a tiny nozzle that shoots a fine spray of paint on to a surface. A small electric motor powers the machine, which is called an airbrush. An airbrush is often used for technical paintings such as cars.

Inventor's words

binder • canvas
paint • pigment
substance
texture

Today, paint is usually mixed in a big vat.

Make a textured cave painting

You will need

- newspaper
- bowl
- flour • building brick
- white paint
- paintbrush
- natural coloring such as soil, charcoal, crushed berries, ketchup, tomato purée

1 Tear up a sheet of newspaper and place in a bowl of water. Add a spoonful of flour. Leave to soak overnight.

2 Squeeze the pulp, then spread a thin layer on the face of the brick to make a rough texture, like the wall of a cave. Leave to dry.

3 Mix a small amount of white paint as the base, then make different colors using natural ingredients.

4 Use your homemade colors to paint a cave painting on the brick. It will make an attractive bookend or doorstop.

How Can I Communicate Over a Long Distance?

Tutenbrodwey loves poetry. As a respected priest, he is allowed to decorate the walls of the temple with his poems. His alphabet is made up of over 2,000 symbols known as hieroglyphics. People come from far and wide to read them.

But Tutenbrodwey is not happy. He wants to show his poems to his friends—but they live a long way away.

There is no way to get the temple walls to his friends. And even if they make the long journey to his temple, they will soon forget the poems after they return home.

How can my friends read my poems if they live far away?

WHAT CAN HE DO?

- Copy the poems on to very small clay tablets and send them out with messengers. But he'd need lots of tablets and lots of messengers.

- Write all over a messenger's body and read the poem as he spins round. Dizzy work!

- Perhaps he could engrave the poems on something lighter—leaves for example.

- Then he noticed how the local papyrus reed was used in homes to make flat mats. Perhaps he could use flat papyrus for his hieroglyphics.

Papyrus reed will work fine. I'll place strips of it in layers, like a mat. Then I'll press them together to make a thin, flat surface. I could even roll up the papyrus mat and carry it around with me.

An Egyptian priest with a papyrus document.

Papyrus

Papyrus is a water plant that grows in Egypt. It has **reed**-like stems that grow up to 9.9 feet (3 m) high. The ancient Egyptians pressed strips from the stem of the plant between boards. The pressure made the fibers mesh together to create long, rectangular sheets of **porous** white writing material.

These sheets were rolled up into **scrolls** and tied with a leather **thong**, a thin strip of animal hide, or cord. The famous library at Alexandria, Egypt's capital, held over 400,000 papyrus scrolls. They dealt with subjects such as astronomy and geography. Some scrolls lasted for thousands of years.

Picture writing

Imagine what the world was like before writing existed. If people wanted to pass on important information, they had to do so by word of mouth. The listener then had to remember it. Writing allows people to store information: written information can be read by someone in a different place or at a different time.

About 6,000 years ago, the people of the ancient Middle Eastern country of Sumer were the first to write down information. They did not use words. Instead, to help remember details of their crops and animals, they scratched pictures called **pictograms** into wet clay. The clay tablets, which were about the size of postcards, became the first kind of stored or portable information, which could be read long after they were written.

PAPER FROM BARK

The kind of paper we know today was invented in China in AD 105. The inventor, Cai Lun, worked in the court of the Chinese Emperor. Cai Lun shredded the inner bark of the mulberry tree into fibers. These were then pressed together to make paper. Later, paper was made from rags, rope, and even shredded fish nets.

Sumerian pictograms marked on a clay tablet.

Inventor's words

information
paper
papyrus
pictogram
porous
reed
scroll
thong

Make your own sheet of paper

Papyrus is made from reeds from the Nile River. You can use a similar method to make paper, using old newspapers.

You will need

- newspaper
- bowl
- wire mesh • old towels
- big plastic bag
- board or old tray
- clean kitchen towel
- scissors • paint

1 Tear up the newspaper into small pieces. Fill a bowl with water. Add the pieces of paper and leave to soak overnight.

2 Place a piece of fine wire mesh in the kitchen sink, and pour a thin layer of newspaper pulp over it.

3 Lift the mesh on to a pile of old towels, cover with a large plastic bag, then press down hard with the board to squeeze out the water.

4 Remove the board, flip the pulp over on to the clean kitchen towel and carefully remove the wire mesh. Leave to dry overnight.

5 Remove the paper from the cloth. Trim your paper into a rectangle, and paint with Egyptian hieroglyphics or make a sign for your room.

Glossary

Aerodynamic Slippery shape that reduces the effect of friction to allow an object to move more easily through the air.

Arm Part of a lever that rests on the fulcrum, or pivot.

Atom Tiniest part of a substance. Atoms are so small that a speck of dust contains a million million atoms.

Axe Type of wedge with a sharp edge that is attached to a handle. It is used for chopping hard materials such as wood.

Axle Rod that fits into the hub, or center, of a wheel.

Binder Sticky substance that is mixed with pigment to adhere paint to a surface.

Blade Sharp part of a plow that cuts through the soil.

Bow Wedge-shaped front of a ship.

Bridge Structure that allows people to pass over a river, valley, road, or railway.

Building Permanent structure in which people can live or work.

Canvas Strong, coarse cloth that artists use for oil paintings.

Compress Press or squeeze something to make it smaller.

Concrete Mixture made up of cement, water, and crushed stone that is used for building.

Crossbeam Horizontal beam made of a strong material that is used to take the weight of a heavy object or building.

Density Ratio of an object's mass (how much matter there is in an object) to its volume. Density is measured in grams per cubic centimeter.

Disc Solid shape that is round, thin, and flat.

Displace Push out of the way. Water can be displaced by a solid object.

Effort A force. The pull or push force that makes things move or change shape.

Expand Become bigger or take up more space. Most gases, liquids, and solids expand when they are heated.

Flint Hard rock found as gray or brown pebbles in chalk and limestone.

Floating To be immersed in water without sinking. An object floats if its weight is less than the weight of the water it displaces.

Force A push or a pull. Forces make things move or change shape.

Friction Rubbing of two moving objects against each other, causing them to slow down and produce heat.

Fulcrum Part of a lever that supports the arm. The rest of the lever pivots or moves around it.

Furrow Narrow cut or groove in the earth made by a plow, into which seeds are sown.

Girder Beam made of strong material such as steel that is used to support parts of a structure.

Gravity Force that pulls objects toward each other. Gravity gives objects weight.

Hieroglyphic Picture writing used by the ancient Egyptians and other early cultures.

Inclined plane Sloping surface.

Inflate Fill with gas or air in order to increase an object's size.

Information Facts that people learn, are told, or that they hear.

Irrigate Take water by ditch or other means to dry land when there is not enough rainfall for crops to grow.

Lever Bar or rod that moves around a fulcrum. The effort of pressing down on one end lifts a load.

Lintel Horizontal piece of timber or stone across the top of a door or window.

Load Weight that a force pushes against. Machines move loads while bridges and beams support them.

Longhouse Single-room building that is longer than it is wide, usually made of wood.

Megalith Large stone used as part of a prehistoric structure.

Monument Structure made for a special occasion or religious reason.

Mortar Mixture of cement, sand, and water used to join bricks or stones together, which strengthens walls.

Paint Material used for coloring objects.

Paper Thin material mostly used for writing on or for printing. It can be made from plant fibers or from rags of cotton or linen.

Papyrus Water plant found on the banks of the Nile River in Egypt. A writing material was made from its stem.

Pictogram Picture used as a symbol in a system of writing.

Pier A bridge support that acts on a force against the stress on the bridge.

Pigment Substance, usually a powder, used to color paint.

Plow Machine with a blade that digs into and turns soil ready for seeds to be sown.

Porous Able to absorb air, water, or other liquids.

Pressure Amount of force pressing down on the surface of an object. Pressure is measured in newtons per square meter.

Raft Simple boat with a flat bottom and no sides usually powered by a pole, oars, or sail.

Ramp Inclined plane or sloping surface.

Reed Water plant with a long stem.

Scroll Length of writing material rolled around a rod or pair of rods. A scroll is unrolled for reading.

Shadoof Simple machine that raises water based on a lever system. It is often used to irrigate fields.

Shelter Building used for protection from the weather, attack, or other phenomena.

Spear Long, aerodynamic pole with a sharp stone or metal blade attached to one end that is used in hunting or warfare.

Stabilize Keep an object firm or fixed so it is not easily moved.

Stilt Long pole used to hold something up or increase its height for protection.

Strain Type of force. A pull that stretches very tightly.

Stress Force that makes an object change its shape. Stress can compress or stretch an object, or make parts of an object slide over each other.

Structure Solid object that encloses, supports, or spans other things.

Substance Any kind of matter, whether a solid, liquid, or gas.

Texture How a substance or the surface of an object feels to the touch.

Thong Thin strip of leather.

Volume Amount of space an object or liquid takes up.

Wedge Piece of material that is thick at one end and tapers to a sharp edge at the other. As a simple machine, it can change the direction of a force and make it stronger.

Wheel Disc that rotates, or turns, around an axle.

Wind tunnel Building that contains a wind-making machine for testing the aerodynamics of objects such as cars and airplanes.

Index

Tools and Materials

Almost all of the materials in this book can be found around the house or bought at your local art or craft shop. If you cannot find the exact item, try and replace it with something similar.

Most of the models will stick fast with craft glue or wallpaper paste. However, some materials need a stronger glue, so be careful when using these as they may damage your clothes and even your skin. Ask an adult to help you.

Always protect furniture with newspaper or a large cloth, and cover your clothes by wearing an apron.

User Care

Take special care when handling sharp tools such as scissors, pointed gadgets, pieces of wire, or craft knives. Ask an adult to help you when you need to use them.

Crafty
Inventions

Crafty
Inventions

Crafty
Inventions

Crafty
Inventions

Crafty
Inventions

Crafty
Inventions

Crafty
Inventions

Crafty
Inventions

Crafty
Inventions